Mammal Babies

Catherine Veitch

Raintree

Raintree is an imprint of Capstone Global Library Limited, a company incorporated in England and Wales having its registered office at 7 Pilgrim Street, London, EC4V 6LB – Registered company number: 6695582

www.raintreepublishers.co.uk
myorders@raintreepublishers.co.uk

Text © Capstone Global Library Limited 2013
First published in hardback in 2013
Paperback edition first published in 2014
The moral rights of the proprietor have been asserted.

Edited by Daniel Nunn, Rebecca Rissman, and Catherine Veitch
Designed by Cynthia Della-Rovere
Picture research by Ruth Blair
Production by Victoria Fitzgerald
Originated by Capstone Global Library
Printed and bound in China

ISBN 978 1 406 25925 4 (hardback)
17 16 15 14 13
10 9 8 7 6 5 4 3 2 1

ISBN 978 1 406 25932 2 (paperback)
18 17 16 15 14
10 9 8 7 6 5 4 3 2 1

British Library Cataloguing in Publication Data
Veitch, Catherine.
Mammal babies. -- (Animal babies)
599.1'39-dc23
A full catalogue record for this book is available from the British Library.

Acknowledgements
We would like to thank the following for permission to reproduce photographs: Corbis p. 10 (© Jenny E. Ross), 19 (© Tim Fitzharris/Minden Pictures); Getty Images pp. 11 (Aurora), 12 (Sumio Harada/Minden Pictures), 15 (Oxford Scientific) 23 (Oxford Scientific); Naturepl pp.5 (© Anup Shah), 6 (© Jane Burton), 7 (© Eric Baccega); 13 (© Steven David Miller), 16 (© Peter Blackwell), 17 (© Anup Shah), 23 (© Anup Shah); Shutterstock pp. title page (© Villiers Steyn), 4 (© Joel Shawn), 8 (© holbox), 9 (© Villiers Steyn), 14 (© Krzysztof Wiktor), 18 (© Lenkadan), 20 (© Kati Molin), 21 (© Flashon Studio), 22 (© Uryadnikov Sergey, © Kitch Bain), 23 (© Flashon Studio).

Front cover photograph of a Bornean orangutan cuddling her baby reproduced with kind permission of Corbis (© Anup Shah).

We would like to thank Michael Bright for his invaluable help in the preparation of this book.

Every effort has been made to contact copyright holders of material reproduced in this book. Any omissions will be rectified in subsequent printings if notice is given to the publisher.

Contents

What is a mammal?

hair

A mammal is an animal with hair or fur.

Female mammals feed their babies milk.

How are baby mammals born?

baby

Most female mammals give birth to babies.

baby seal

Some mammals have one baby at a time.

Some mammals have many babies at a time.

Most baby mammals look like
their parents.

Where do baby mammals live?

den

Baby mammals need a safe place
to live. Many baby mammals live
in dens.

burrow

Many baby mammals live in burrows.

nest

Many baby mammals live in nests.

pouch

Some baby mammals live in their
mothers' pouches.

Caring for baby mammals

Many mammals lick their babies' fur to keep it clean.

Many mammals protect their
babies from predators.

Many mammals teach their babies
to hunt.

Many mammals teach their babies
to fight.

Many mammal babies stay with their mothers for a long time.

Some mammals are looked after
by both parents.

Humans are mammals, too.

Human babies need a lot of help from adults.

Life cycle of a mammal

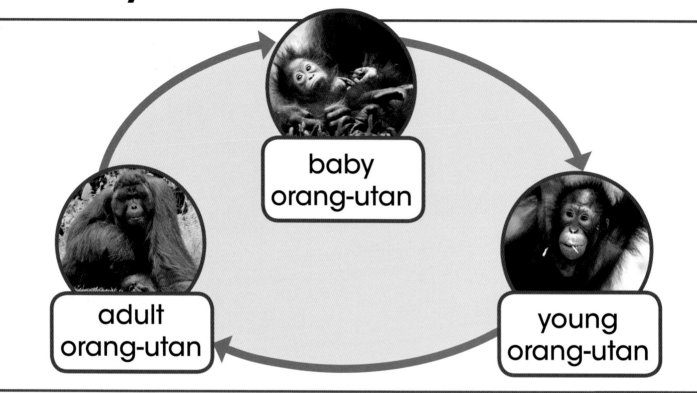

baby orang-utan

adult orang-utan

young orang-utan

A life cycle shows the different stages of an animal's life. This is the life cycle of an orang-utan.

Picture glossary

adult grown-up. A child grows into an adult.

female animal that can give birth. Female mammals feed their babies milk from their bodies.

predator animal that eats other animals

Index

Notes for parents and teachers

Before reading

Show children a collection of photos and videos of mammals. National Geographic and BBC Nature are useful websites. Explain what a mammal is and discuss the characteristics of mammals.

After reading

- Mount photos of adult and baby mammals on card, and play games of snap and pairs where the children have to match a baby mammal with its parent. Model the correct pairs first.

- Ask children to label the parts of a mammal: for example, fur, legs, tail, ears.

- Look at page 22 and discuss the life cycle stages of a mammal. Mount photos of the baby, young and adult stages and ask children to put the photos in order. Encourage children to draw a life cycle of a human to compare. Compare how different mammals care for their babies. Discuss the care human babies need.

- To extend children's knowledge, the mammals are as follows: zebra: p4; impala and fawn: p5; horse and foal: p6; seal and pup: p7; dog and puppies: p8; elephant and calf: p9; polar bear cubs: p10; kittens (baby rabbits): p11; kittens (baby squirrels): p12; kangaroo and joey: p13; lioness and cub: p14; bear and cubs: p15; cheetah and cub: p16; infant baboons: p17; horse and foal: p18; wolves and cub: p19.